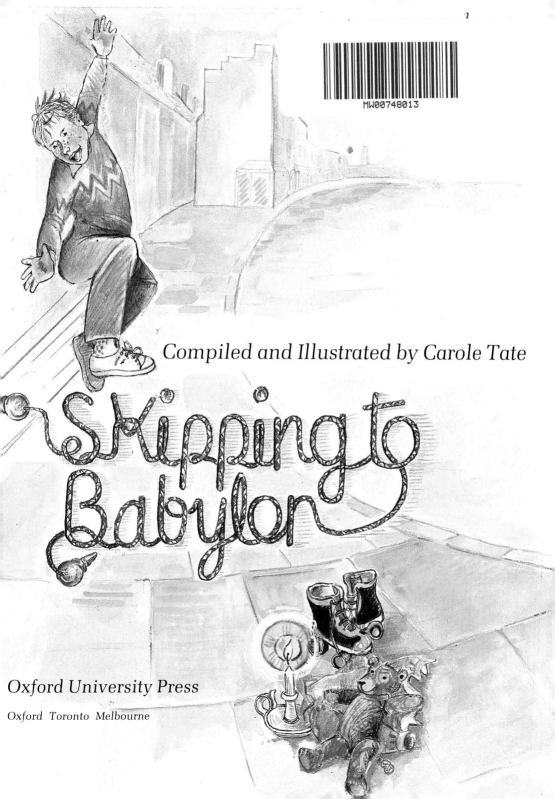

Compiled and Illustrated by Carole Tate

Skipping to Babylon

Oxford University Press

Oxford Toronto Melbourne

Oxford University Press, Walton Street, Oxford OX2 6DP

Oxford London
New York Toronto Melbourne Auckland
Kuala Lumpur Singapore Hong Kong Tokyo
Delhi Bombay Calcutta Madras Karachi
Nairobi Dar es Salaam Cape Town

and associated companies in
Beirut Berlin Ibadan Mexico City Nicosia

Oxford is a trade mark of Oxford University Press

© Carole Tate 1985
An Umbrella Book *Series Editor:* Jill Bennett
First published 1985

British Library Cataloguing in Publication Data
Tate, Carole
  Skipping to Babylon.—(Umbrella Books)
  1. Jump rope rhymes
  I. Title
  398′.8 PZ8.3
  ISBN 0-19-278206-1

Typeset by Oxford Publishing Services
Printed in Hong Kong

How many miles to Babylon?
Three score and ten, sir.
Can I get there by candlelight?
Oh, yes, and back again, sir.
If your heels are nimble and light,
You may get there by candlelight.

I had a little brother,
His name was Tiny Tim.
I put him in the bathtub
To teach him how to swim.
He drank up all the water,
He ate up all the soap,
He died last night
With a bubble in his throat.

In came the doctor,
In came the nurse,
In came the lady,
With the alligator purse.
'Death,' said the doctor.
'Death,' said the nurse.
'Death,' said the lady
With the alligator purse.

Out went the doctor,
Out went the nurse,
Out went the lady
With the alligator purse.

Spin a coin, spin a coin,
   All fall down.
Queen Nefertiti
Stalks through the town.

Over the pavements her feet go clack.

Her legs are as tall as a chimney stack.

Her fingers flicker like snakes in the air,
The walls split open at her green-eyed stare.

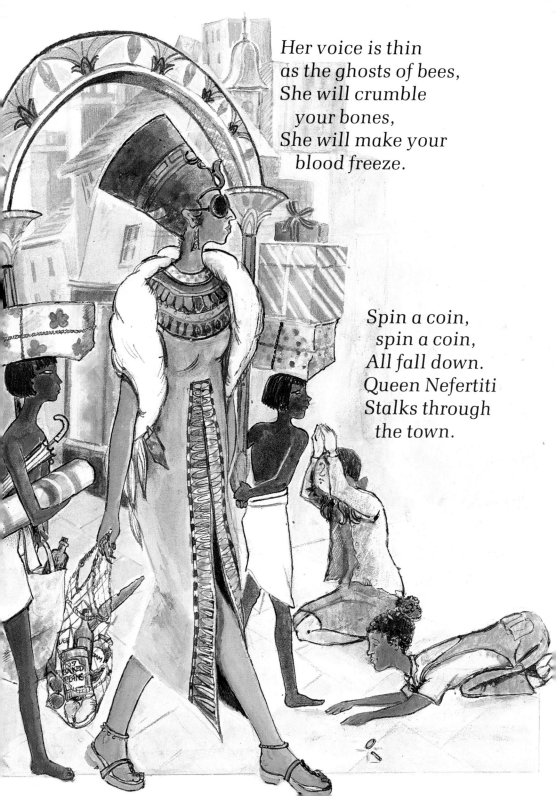

Her voice is thin
as the ghosts of bees,
She will crumble
  your bones,
She will make your
  blood freeze.

Spin a coin,
  spin a coin,
All fall down.
Queen Nefertiti
Stalks through
  the town.

Salt, Mustard, Vinegar, Pepper,
  French Almond Rock.
Bread and butter for your supper
That's all mother's got.
Fish and chips and Coca Cola,
Pig's head and trout.
Bread and butter for your supper,

O.U.T. spells out.

The big ship sails on the Alley, Alley O,
The Alley, Alley O, the Alley, Alley O.
The big ship sails on the Alley, Alley O,
On the last day of September.

The Captain said: 'It will never, never do, etc.

The big ship sank to the bottom of the sea, etc.

We all dip our heads in the
    deep, blue sea,
The deep, blue sea, the deep,
    blue sea,
We all dip our heads in the
    deep, blue sea,
On the last day of September.

The Ladies of the Harem
of the Court of King Caractacus
were just passing by.

Oh, the Ladies of the Harem
of the Court of King Caractacus
were just passing by.

The noses on the Ladies of the Harem
of the Court of King Caractacus
were just passing by.

The boys who put the powder on the noses
of the Ladies of the Harem
of the Court of King Caractacus
were just passing by.
The fascinating witches who put the
scintillating stitches in the breeches
of the boys who put the powder on the noses
of the Ladies of the Harem
of the Court of King Caractacus
were just passing by.

If you want to see
the fascinating witches
who put the scintillating stitches
in the breeches of the boys
who put the powder on the noses
of the Ladies of the Harem
of the Court of King Caractacus—
You're too late!
They've just passed by.

Salome was a dancer,
She danced the hootchie cootch.
She shook her shimmy shoulder,
And showed a bit too much.
'Stop!' said King Herod,
'You can't do that there 'ere.'
Salome said, 'Baloney!'
And she kicked the chandelier.

I like coffee, I like tea,
I like the boys and they like me.
So tell your ma to hold her tongue
'Cos she had a boy when she was young.
And tell your pa to do the same,
'Cos he was the one who changed her name.

Nebuchadnezzar
the King of the Jews
sold his wife
for a pair of shoes.

When the shoes began to wear

Nebuchadnezzar began to swear.

When the shoes got worse and worse
Nebuchadnezzar began to curse.

When the shoes were quite worn out
Nebuchadnezzar began to shout.

When the shouting began to stop
Nebuchadnezzar bought a shop.
When the shop began to sell
Nebuchadnezzar bought a bell.

When the bell began to ring
Nebuchadnezzar began to sing.
Doh, Ray, Me, Fa, So, La, Tee, Doh.

Here's to the poor widow from Babylon
With six poor children all alone.
One can bake and one can brew,
One can shape and one can sew,
One can sit at the fire and spin,
One can bake a cake for the King.
Come choose you east, come choose you west,
Come choose the one that you love best.

*If your heels be nimble and light,
You may get there by candlelight.*